Organizational Design and Structure, Employee Pay and Compensation, Employee Reviews, and Absenteeism.
4 books on employees and organizations in 1

Louis Bevoc

Published by
NutriNiche System LLC

Louis Bevoc books...simple explanations of complex subjects

Organizational Design and Structure	3
Employee Pay and Compensation	18
Employee Reviews	33
Absenteeism	48

Organizational Design and Structure
Describing and Exemplifying

Louis Bevoc

Published by
NutriNiche System LLC

Louis Bevoc books...simple explanations of complex subjects

Introduction — 5
- Organizational design — 5
- Organizational structure — 5

Design determination — 5
- Division of jobs — 6
- Division of departments — 6
- Division of authority — 7

Design types — 8
- Simple structure — 8
- Matrix structure — 9
- Bureaucratic structure — 11
- Virtual structure — 13

Design differences — 15
- Strategy — 15
- Size — 16
- Age — 16
- Technology — 16
- Environment — 16

Summary — 16

Introduction

Organization design and structure define workplace culture. They work together to define management style, establish the working environment, and accomplish the goals and objectives of the organization. They also make sure that work related tasks are completed in an accurate and timely manner.

While design and structure intertwine to create culture, they do have some differences. These differences are as follows:

Organizational design

Design involves management choices that integrate people and processes to accomplish organizational goals and objectives. It is the management style used to support the organizational structure.

Organizational structure

Structure defines the formal authority in an organization, as well as the roles that employees assume. It focuses on the systems in place to create a working environment.

Organizations can be structured in a variety of ways depending on established goals and objectives. This structure is important because it provides a roadmap of how the organization operates as a whole. It also defines the roles and responsibilities of people and departments, and it indicates decision making power and processes.

In order to be effective, organizational structure depends on three major factors. These are:

Management

Management must properly position employees to accomplish work related tasks.

Employees

Employees must have the necessary skills to accomplish work related tasks.

Processes and procedures

Processes and procedures must create positive work flow to accomplish work related tasks.

As noted earlier, organizational design supports organizational structure. That design is established using certain components of the organization, and the next section will show how this is done.

Design determination

Design is the management style used to support organizational structure. However, questions about the design need to be answered before it can be determined. These questions stem from the following:

Division of jobs

This is where work in the organization is divided into separate jobs. Essentially, all work can be broken down into procedural steps, and those steps are completed by individual employees. The idea here is that employees specialize in doing part of the work, rather than all of it.

This means that employees will have different skills for the jobs they perform. Management directs employees to use their skills in designated areas, and the organization becomes more efficient. For example, an automotive assembly line has many separate jobs. There is a different employee for every step of the process until the finished product is completed. This is much more efficient than having every employee assemble a car by themselves. Additionally, the cost for specialized employee training at one step of the process is much less than the cost of training an employee to build an entire car.

Division of departments

After jobs have been divided, they need to be grouped into departments so they can be coordinated. This is typically done using one of the following three major categories:

Product

In this category, departments are determined based on products. For example, a grocery store might have the following departments:

> Meat – sausage, hamburger, steak, and ham
> Dairy – Yogurt, milk, ice cream, and cheese
> Bakery – bagels, bread, donuts, and pastries

Service

In this category, departments are determined based on services. For example, an outdoor maintenance company might have the following departments:

> Lawn care – mowing, edging, weeding, and fertilizing grass
> Pest control – Bird, rodent, bug, and insect control
> Landscaping – Trees, bushes, shrubs, and other outdoor decor

Function

In this category, departments are determined based on functions. For example, a stamping plant might have the following departments:

> Quality assurance – product quality and specification monitoring

Human resources – personnel and benefits administration
Accounting – bookkeeping and financial transactions

Division of authority

After departments have been created, authority over those departments needs to be established. This is typically done using a chain of command with specific authority for each manager in the chain. This streamlines productivity and prevents the confusion that results when employees report to multiple bosses.

Two major factors that need to be taken into account when establishing division of authority are:

Levels of management

Organizations need to determine the ratio of managers to employees. Higher ratios mean more levels of management, and lower levels mean fewer levels of management. Often times, levels of management are based on the skills of the employees. Highly skilled employees typically need less supervision, and this means the organization has fewer management levels. Conversely, employees with low skills often need closer supervision, so there are more management levels in these organizations.

Centralized vs. decentralized decision making

In centralized organizations, upper management makes all of the decisions. Lower level managers simply make sure the decisions are implemented. An example of centralized management is the military during a war. Generals make decisions, and those decisions are carried out by lower ranking staff.

An advantage of centralized decision making over decentralized decision making is there is more assurance that the directives of top management will be implemented. Think about the Catholic Church. The Pope makes decisions that are very likely to be carried out by lower ranking members of the organization.

Decentralized organizations give power to managers at the lower levels. An example is a sports team. The coach is the lowest level of management, but he or she is closest to the action and has the authority to make changes on the spot.

An advantage of decentralized decision making over centralized decision making is reaction time to problems is much quicker. Think about Alcoholics Anonymous. Each chapter or division is run by local members with no formal direction from a higher level of management. Ideals and goals are present, but they are organized and carried out at the lowest levels.

Now you understand how organizational structures are designed. In the next section, we will examine some of the more common design types.

Design types

It would very be difficult to describe every type of organizational design in the world. However, there are common organizational designs that can be discussed for better understanding. Please consider the following design types:

Simple structure

A simple structure has limited departments, limited levels of management, and centralized decision making. This structure is flexible and cost effective, and management responsibilities are typically laid out well.

In many small businesses, there is only one level of management. That level contains one person...the owner. The owner acts as the centralized decision maker for every aspect of the business, and he or she also performs a variety of other job functions when necessary. Below are some strengths and weaknesses of a simple structure:

Strengths

This type of organizational design works well for small businesses when the owner understands the need of the organization. He or she knows what is best for the business, and that allows him or her to make the right choices. Additionally, employees do not question business decisions because they come from the top of the organization. Finally, there is limited miscommunication because decisions do not have to be filtered thought multi-levels of management. Fewer levels of management also allow for faster implementation of ideas and concepts.

Organizational example

Jack founded a small appliance store 12 years ago, and he is activity involved in the business. He makes all major business decisions and runs every aspect of the company. He has survived hard times and economic downturns because he understands his business well.

Jack employs six people at his store. One person answers phones and runs the office, one rotates stock, and the other three are salespeople. Essentially, there is only one level of management (supervision - Jack). The other employees are simply workers.

All six employees communicate with Jack on a daily basis so mistakes and misunderstandings are rare. They also respect the business decisions he makes based on his knowledge and experience.

Jacks designed his business to be a simple structure, and this has worked well for him for many years.

Weaknesses

One problem is with simple structures is the organization can be in big trouble if the only decision maker gets sick, retires, or dies. No one else is capable of making decisions, and this puts the organization in limbo.

Another problem is that some decision makers have difficultly delegating authority as the organization grows. There comes a point when one person simply cannot make every decision, and others are not capable or do not have the authority to do so.

Finally, a few poor decisions by one individual can jeopardize the well-being of the company and its employees. Everyone makes mistakes, but a major decision maker's choices are critical and rarely challenged...and this can be devastating.

Organizational example

Martha owns a small electrical distribution company. She understands the electrical business well, and she makes every major decision that affects the company.

Over the past year, Martha's company has experienced rapid growth. She picked up three major accounts, and the companies' sales have more than tripled. Based on this increase in volume, Martha has had to expand her workforce from eight employees to 26.

The sales expansion experienced by the electrical distribution company is good for business, but it has also caused some problems. Martha is more involved with sales than she ever was in the past, and she no longer has the proper time to manage the day-to-day operations. Combine this with the fact that her workforce has more than tripled, and the business is simply too much for her to handle. Other employees are capable of making decisions, but Martha is unwilling to delegate authority to them, and she will not listen to anyone who tells her to relinquish some of her power.

Martha's inability to delegate authority is causing the business to suffer. She needs to change the design of the business from a simple structure to something a bit more complex, but she does not want to do this and will not listen to anyone who advises her to do so.

Matrix structure

Employees often need to work together in order to complete projects, and sometimes this requires two bosses. A matrix allows employees to have a product manager and a functional department manager (a dual chain of command). This is often implemented in organizations that need to share information between departments in order to resolve problems.

Matrix structures work well in certain organizations, but they not as common as a simple structure or bureaucracy. Organizations need to weight the advantages and disadvantages of design type before making a decision to implement it. Below are some strengths and weaknesses of a matrix structure:

Strengths

A matrix works well for large organizations with complex interdependent activities...such as universities or government agencies. Communication can be greatly improved and people are able to receive information faster due to structural flexibility. This leads to faster decision making and problem resolution, and it results in improved productivity and better customer satisfaction

Organizational example

Jane works as a designer for a home remodeling company. Her newest responsibility is to design quality kitchen cabinets out of plastic that resembles wood. The plastic is much less expensive and durable than wood, but it looks "cheap" or "tacky" in some kitchens.

For this project, Jane needs to answer to two different bosses She answers to the manager of the accounting department to a assure costs are where they need to be, and she answers to the marketing director to make sure customers will like the design.

The structural arrangement Jane is working under works well because she receives immediate feedback from important people about her cabinet design. The project gets completed in less than one week, and it meets quality and cost specifications. In this case, a matrix structure worked well for Jane and the home remodeler.

Weaknesses

The problem with a matrix is it creates stress and uncertainty since people are not always sure whom they report to in the organization. This can create confusion and establish warring factions in the midst of power struggles. The confusion can result in frustrated employees and high turnover rates.

Matrix structures often do not work well in assembly or production environments. Production jobs are very predictable, and the employees perform best when they answer to one boss who gives them the direction needed to accomplish work related tasks.

When thinking about a matrix, it must be remembered that improper implementation can have a negative effect on employee motivation and morale due to the lack of structure. This is rather ironic because the goal of a matrix is to provide structure and make it easier to achieve organizational goals.

Organizational example

Rafael works in sales for a Safeco, an organization that sells safety equipment to companies that handle dangerous chemicals.

Safeco has recently developed a face shield that is virtually indestructible. It will not break or melt under even the most severe conditions, and it is of substantial value to some of their customers.

Rafael wants to sell the face shield, but in order to do so, he needs to answer to two different bosses. The sales manager Peggy wants to get the product out in the field, and she tells Rafael to offer it below cost to get it moving. The COO Timothy wants the item to be highly profitable, and he tells Rafael to sell it at a 30 percent markup.

The discrepancy between Peggy and Timothy causes confusion for Rafael because he is not sure what price the face shield should be offered to customers. Worse yet, Peggy and Timothy are fighting at the office about who has the authority to establish pricing.

One week later, there is no resolution to the problem. Timothy and Peggy are still arguing, and no price has been established. Rafael becomes discouraged and begins to look for new employment. In this case, the matrix structure caused confusion and fighting, and it did not work well for Rafael or Safeco.

Bureaucratic structure

Organizations with bureaucratic structures are typically very inflexible. They have written rules and regulations in place that are upheld by the employees exactly as defined. Clearly established hierarchies, centralized decision making, and divisions of labor are present at all times. As might be expected, standardized processes and procedures are the norms.

It takes monumental time and effort to change bureaucracies due to the rules involved and the strict chain-of-command protocol. Because of this, people often cringe at the thought of dealing with a bureaucracy in order to implement something new...and city government is a good example. People who want cities to change often face a mountain of a task. This is why the phrase "you can't change city hall" has become so well known.

Below are some strengths and weaknesses of a bureaucratic structure:

Strengths

Bureaucracies have some advantages over other structures. They are very efficient at performing standardized actions. Activities are performed following the same protocol every time, and this allows employees to become very good at their jobs while adhering to safety and quality standards. Additionally, rigid rules and regulations allow less competent lower level managers to be part of the workforce because there is little need for them to make important decisions.

Bureaucratic structures are very important for many United States governmental agencies. They need well documented rules and regulation in place to make sure the law is being adhered to in the proper manner. Bureaucracies also add assurance that all people are being treated equally, and this is important for democracy.

Organizational example

Jonathon is a firefighter at a fire department operated by a large metropolitan city. The department has strict procedures in place for every fire to avoid chaos and provide safety for the firefighters.

One of the procedures states that firefighters are not allowed to enter buildings that are on fire because the structures could collapse due to the heat and damage. During a recent warehouse fire, Jonathon started to go inside to yell for any people that might be trapped. His boss immediately stopped him because this action does not comply with standard procedures. Three minutes after Jonathon's boss prevented him from entering the building, it collapsed. If Jonathon had gone inside, he likely would have been killed.

In this particular case, the bureaucratic structure in place was successful because a specific protocol was followed. Jonathon was not allowed to deviate from procedure for safety reasons, and this likely ended up saving his life.

Weaknesses

Disadvantages to bureaucratic structures include (1) they are slow to react to problems and (2) they are difficult to change. Along the same lines, employees within these organizations are fixated on following the rules exactly. They do not deviate from standard procedures, and anything that does not adhere to established regulations is rejected or put on hold. Common sense rarely comes into play because employees do not like to leave their comfort zones.

A bureaucratic structure does not work for creative organizations. A technology based company, for example, would falter under bureaucracy because it would defeat the organization's entire purpose of being innovative.

Organizational example

Michelle works for the United States Department of Agriculture (USDA) as a Consumer Safety Inspector. Her job is to police meat and poultry processing establishments to assure that they are conforming to USDA regulatory standards.

One of the standards in the USDA regulations states that production floors "must be maintained in a sanitary manner and free of debris in order to prevent food safety hazards." Michelle walks into a 100,000 square foot meat processing plant and finds one hairnet on the floor by one of the doors leading into a production area. She documents non-compliance for this hairnet stating that the floor is not free of debris, and therefore not maintained in a sanitary manner.

Michelle's non-compliance infuriates the plant manager. He argues that the floor is spotless except for this one hairnet, and this does not create an unsanitary condition nor does it present any type of food safety hazard. Michelle will not listen to the plant manager's complaint. She follows the rules exactly and does not allow any room for deviation.

In this particular case, the bureaucracy failed. One hairnet on a 100,000 square foot floor does not make it unsanitary, nor does it present any type of food safety hazard. Michelle refused to use common sense because this would have taken her out of her comfort zone by requiring her to deviate from standard procedures. The end result was a documented non-compliance for no legitimate reason.

Virtual structure

Virtually structured organizations are fairly unique. Employees do not share office space, communication is electronic or phone based, and knowledge is much more important than physical assets. Online dating services and auction houses are examples of organizations that can be virtually structured.

Some of the more interesting characteristics of virtual structures include:

Outsourcing

This is by no means a new concept, but virtual organizations typically outsource most of their work. This makes them much more efficient because specialists can be brought in on an "as needed" basis.

Departments

Virtual organizations generally have no need for departments because most jobs are outsourced and do not need to be coordinated. This limits miscommunication and allows for faster decision making.

Decision making

Decision making in virtual organizations is highly centralized. One person often makes the decisions for the entire organization, and that one person might be the only level of management.

Change

Virtual organizations are very open to change and constantly evolving. This is because they are typically small in size with limited levels of management.

Longevity

Virtual organizations are often assembled for the short term. They cease to exist as soon as a project as finished. This is relatively easy to do since they outsource much of their work and employ few employees. An example includes an organization set up to raise money for the medical needs of a sick child.

In short, virtual organizations are essentially the opposite of bureaucracies. They are very flexible with few rules and regulations. They also need competent employees for management positions because important decisions need to be made.

Below are some strengths and weaknesses of a virtual structure:

Strengths

One advantage of a virtual organization is cost savings. Time and travel expenses are reduced or eliminated since people can communicate from anywhere in the world. This benefits employees in terms of work-life balance, and it also positively impacts the organization's bottom line.

Another advantage involves hiring. There are essentially no geographical boundaries when hiring employees, so the best people can be brought on board. An example includes a virtual college that wants to hire all doctoral level professors as faculty. They have the entire world to choose from for the selection process. Conversely, a traditional university might only be able to hire doctoral candidates within a 50-mile radius of the campus…and this is much more restricting.

Organizational example

Donna works as a website designer for a company located in Arizona. She lives in Texas and is able to complete work with customers all over the world without ever leaving her house. Lately, she has been doing work for several companies located in Brazil, and they are very happy with her service and performance. When she completes a job for one company, they recommend her to another Brazilian firm.

In Donna's situation, a virtual structure works well. She does not need to be physically present at her company's office, and she is able to work from home with customers all over the world. This provides her with good work-life balance, and the organization saves on travel expenses.

Weaknesses

One disadvantage of a virtual organization involves communication since it is mostly done through writing (some phone conversations, but writing is more the norm). The written word (email, text, or letter) works well in many situations, but it can also be easily misinterpreted. Most people who have worked with email understand this dilemma, and they realize that some communication requires face-to-face human interaction. Non-verbal communication, body language, and paralanguage (voice quality, tempo, loudness, and vocal features) are all important for relaying the meaning of messages, and face-to-face contact generally is needed for achieving the full effect. If face-to-face communication is not possible, then employees can lose the ability to effectively communicate. Time is also wasted as people work towards understanding the messages being sent.

Another disadvantage to virtual structures involves hours of work. Employees live in different time zones all over the world, and this makes it difficult to hold meetings or discuss issues "live" online. Meetings might need to be held at 2:00 am for some people, and they simply are not at their best when they should be sleeping. Email can be used for employees to answer questions at their convenience, but this slows response time and hinders productivity.

Organizational example

Marcus is employed at a computer software company as a troubleshooter for computer systems. His job affords him the luxury of working full time out of his home office. For the most part, this works out very well for Marcus. However, it is challenging when he is assigned to a team project.

Currently, Marcus is on a team project with three other employees who physically work at the office. They email back and forth to exchange ideas and information, but sometimes it is hard to understand the true meaning of the messages being sent. For example, Marcus sent out an email with some mild sarcasm that was intended to be humorous and harmless, but one of the team members was offended by it. This created unnecessary stress in the group, and productivity came to a halt until it was resolved with a series of other emails.

Eventually, the team was able to achieve the objectives established by management, but the time needed for completion was twice as much as originally anticipated due to miscommunication. This led management to decide that Marcus will no longer be placed on any teams as long as he works remotely.

The decision to avoid placing Marcus on teams negatively impacts the computer software company because they lose the benefit of his problem solving knowledge. In this particular situation, the virtual structure was not good for the organization.

Now you understand the common types of designs that make up organizational structures. Let's move forward and discuss the reasons designs differ.

Design differences

Why aren't all organizational designs the same? What causes them to differ? These are both good questions, and the following factors provide some insight into the answers:

Strategy

Organizational goals and objectives drive strategies, so it's not surprising that strategies influence design.

Some organizations' strategies revolve around performing basic functions, such as accounting or engineering. Employees, such as accountants and engineers, have specialized expertise in specific areas. In these situations, division of departments is important for the design so employees can focus on specific job functions. The departments are then coordinated by management to accomplish the overall objectives of the organization.

Other organizations' strategies revolve around customer service. Restaurants and hospitals are good examples. These companies sell consumers products or services, and their designs are based on customer needs. Departments are also needed here, but they are based on products or services.

Last, but not least, some organizations' strategies are based on innovation. Web design companies and advertising agencies are good examples. In this case, they need a design that favors flexibility and decentralized decision making. Bureaucratic designs do not work well here because they are far too rigid.

In short, strategies are formulated based on the goals and objectives of the organization. When goals and objectives change, so do strategies. When strategies change, they influence the design that makes up the structure.

Size

The size of an organization also impacts design. Large organizations are different than small ones in terms of division of authority (more levels of management), division of departments (more departments), and division of jobs (more specialized skills). They also differ in terms of goals and objectives.

The most interesting point about size is that it affects design less as organizations grow. Think about it...adding 50 employees to a company with 50 employees has a huge impact on design, but adding 50 employees to a company with 500 employees has much less of an impact.

Age

As organizations mature, they typically become more standardized, specialized, and rule oriented. This changes the goals and objectives of the organization, and those changes affect organizational design.

Technology

Technology includes the knowledge, procedures, and resources needed to produce a product or service. Essentially, this encompasses everything involved during the conversion of inputs to outputs. As technology changes, so does the organization's design.

Environment

Environment impacts decision making. In difficult times, decision making can change...and this influences the design of the organization.

Summary

Workplace culture is determined by organizational design and structure. These two concepts work together to accomplish the goals and objectives of the organization. Along the way, they define management style, establish the working environment, and make sure that work related tasks are completed in an accurate and timely manner.

This book focuses on organizational design and organizational structure. First, the difference between the two concepts is defined. Next determination of design is discussed. Then common design types are explained. Finally, factors that affect design differences are explored.

Congratulations! You now understand organizational design and structure…two very important aspects of organizational behavior.

Employee Pay and Compensation In Organizations
Types, Advantages, and Disadvantages

Louis Bevoc

Published by
NutriNiche System LLC

Louis Bevoc books...simple explanations of complex subjects

Introduction 20
Types 20
    Salary 20
    Hourly 21
    Commission 22
    Bonus 23
    Piece-rate 24
    Merit 25
    Skill 26
    Profit sharing 27
    Gain sharing 28
    Employee stock ownership 29
    Benefits 30
    Work-life balance 31
Summary 32

Introduction

Some people do not need to work. They are financially independent and do not need to earn additional income to live within the means of their current lifestyle. Unfortunately, this is not the case for the majority of the population. Most people need to earn money so they can provide for themselves and their families.

People who do work tend to put a high priority on their compensation. This compensation can come in many different forms including pay, bonuses, commission, retirement plans, profit sharing, stock ownership, and benefits. Employees want job satisfaction, and money always seems to play a role in finding that satisfaction. In fact, money is typically one of the most important aspects of employment, and it is a major reason why workers remain at their current employer or leave for other positions.

This focus of this book is employee pay and compensation in organizations. It examines various types of pay structures and benefits. Specifically, it looks at salary pay, hourly pay, commission pay, bonus pay, piece-rate pay, merit pay, skill pay, profit sharing programs, gain sharing programs, employee stock ownership programs, work-life balance programs, and benefit packages. Each type of compensation is described, discussed in terms of pros and cons, and illustrated using a workplace example.

Let's move into the next section to discuss the types of pay and compensation mentioned above.

Types

This section is the main focus of this book. It discusses employee pay and compensation using workplace examples for illustration and real world application. The writing is rather easy to follow and comprehend, but please note that the advantages and disadvantages are based on the employee rather than the employer. Employer advantages and disadvantages are generally different depending on the situation.

The following are the various types of pay and compensation noted in the introduction:

Salary

This type of pay involves a set amount of money for a certain period of time. Typically, the money is based on one year of work. This wage does not normally change until management decides a change is justified. Usually, employees' salaries go up based on their increased value to the organization. However, salaries can also go down if management believes employees are not producing enough to warrant their wage.

Organizational example

Rocco is a store manager at a submarine sandwich shop. His job is to manage all aspects of the business for a fixed wage that is paid every Friday. He does not have set hours that he has to be at the store, but he needs to make sure it is operating efficiently every day. In short, Rocco receives a weekly salary as compensation for his job responsibilities regardless of the number of hours he works.

Below are some pros and cons of salary pay:

Employee advantages

- Salaried employees are not required to punch a time clock. There is no need to track every minute worked due to the expectations involved. Salaried workers have a job that needs to get done, and, within reason, management will not interfere if it is getting done.

- Salaried employees can easily budget their expenses because they know what they are getting paid. They do not have to wait to see how many hours they worked in a given week or worry about making less money during slow periods.

- Salaried employees experience high job satisfaction. Workers sometimes associate salary with prestige since this is the most common type of compensation for management personnel in organizations. Hourly employees often rank lower in the hierarchy, and they perceive salaried positions as promotions.

Employee disadvantages

- Salaried employees do not get paid overtime when they work more than 40 hours a week. In this respect, they can be taken advantage of by management when they are told they need to complete a job regardless of the time it takes.

- Salaried employees can go long periods of time without pay increases. There are typically no unions to guarantee more money, and management is not required to give raises.

- Salaried employees often have higher work-loads than hourly employees. Salaries are a fixed cost…meaning they get paid out regardless of organizational sales. During slow periods, salaried personnel might be perceived as not doing enough work to support their wage, so management adds more responsibilities to their jobs.

Hourly

Employees who are compensated hourly receive an agreed upon amount of money per hour of work. There is no guaranteed amount of money that these employees make in a year because the number of hours worked depends on organizational needs or customer demand. However, unions have changed the rules for many workplaces by guaranteeing minimum hours per week for hourly employees.

Typically increases in money per hour for hourly employees are based on time intervals or the ability to perform certain job functions. Again, unions have intervened and implemented rules that need to be followed in some workplaces. These rules guarantee employees wage increases after a certain amount of time with the organization. Rarely do hourly wages go down, but this can happen if concessions are implemented.

Organizational example

Katrina is a production worker at a forklift assembly plant, and she earns 14 dollars per hour. When she works over 40 hours in a week, she receives 21 dollars per hour. In short, Katrina's compensation is a pre-determined wage for every hour she works assembling forklifts.

Below are some pros and cons of hourly pay:

Employee advantages

- Hourly employees get paid overtime (typically 1.5 times their normal hourly wage) when they work more than 40 hours a week...and sometimes when they work more than eight hours a day. In this respect, they get paid for every minute they are on the job.

- In general, hourly employees have designated pay increases. For example, management might give them a raise after 90 days to show that they are valued. Unions are often used to guarantee higher wages for these workers, and management has no choice other than to comply once changes in compensation have been negotiated.

- Hourly workers often have less stressful jobs than salaried workers. They have designated work that they must perform, but that work is done under controlled conditions with established productivity requirements.

Employee disadvantages

- Hourly employees are usually required to punch a time clock. Every minute that they work is tracked, and they do not get paid if they are not punched in.

- Hourly employees find it difficult to budget their expenses because they do not know how much money they will earn in a pay period. They have to wait to see how many hours they worked and be concerned about making less money during slow periods.

- Hourly employees lack power. They often rank low in the hierarchy, and they have limited say in the direction of the organization. This can cause job dissatisfaction and lower morale.

Commission

Commission pay is typically used for salespeople. Often times it involves a base salary plus a commission that is based on the total sales achieved. In short, increases sales result in increased commission.

Commission does not necessarily have to be monetary. Depending on the leadership of the organization, it can also be used for purchasing:

- A company vehicle
- An upgrade of a benefit package
- Additional time off or vacation
- A contribution to a retirement plan
- Company stock

Organizational example

Bert is employed as a salesperson for a solar energy company. He receives a base salary, and he gets two percent of his total sales volume as commission. Last year, Bert's sales were $2,000,000, and this resulted in a $40,000 commission for him.

Below are some pros and cons of commission pay:

Employee advantages

- Commission employees are motivated because they are rewarded for reaching goals.

- Commission allows employees the opportunity to live more comfortably. Many organizations have commission plans in place that can be very lucrative for salespeople.

- Commission employees can earn more than their salary without receiving a raise. In this respect, they control some of their own destiny in terms of income.

Employee disadvantages

- Employees who do not achieve commission based goals can end up demotivated. Their efforts are not rewarded, and this can lower their morale.

- Some employees cannot live comfortably without their commission pay. Since organizations want salespeople to perform, they tend to make it difficult for them to survive off only their base pay.

- Employees control some of their financial destiny with commission, but management is watching their earnings closely. If salespeople begin to earn too much money, some organizations lower their commission rates.

Bonus

Bonus pay is money given to people at the end of a specific amount of time. It is typically based on performance, and there are a variety of ways to calculate the amount of money paid out. The bonus can be a percentage of employees' pay, an amount based on the profitability of the organization, a number based on employees' goal achievements, or an arbitrary figure determined by management. Regardless of the method used for determination of the dollar value, the objective of a bonus is to reward employees with additional income.

Organizational example

Tabitha has worked as a nurse in a doctor's office for the past six years. She earns a competitive salary, but the main reason she stays at this office is her year-end bonus. Doctors distribute bonuses to every employee based on their length of service with the organization.

Below are some pros and cons of bonus pay:

Employee advantages

- Bonuses motivate employees by providing a "carrot at the end of the stick." This opportunity for reward entices people to work harder to achieve goals.

- Bonuses can be paid to teams. This is good because every member shares in the success of the group, and it promotes teamwork throughout the organization.

- Bonuses are a nice yearly addition to income...especially if they come during the holidays when they are needed.

Employee disadvantages

- Bonuses are motivating due to the "carrot at the end of the stick", but the size of the "carrot" makes a difference. Employees who receive smaller amounts than expected can actually be demotivated by this added compensation.

- Bonuses based on team accomplishments can cause problems because some members do more work than others. If social loafers get the same bonus as everyone else on the team, then the members who did the majority of the work can become resentful.

- Employees often take bonuses for granted, and they become upset if they do not receive them...even though management does not make any guarantees.

Piece-rate

This form of compensation pays employees a pre-determined amount of money for a specific amount of work. People earn income based on their total output regardless of the amount of time they spend doing the job.

Organizational example

Gary works as an assembler at a cell phone company. He does not receive an hourly wage or a salary for his efforts. Instead, his entire compensation is based on the number of cell phones he assembles, regardless of the amount time it takes him.

Below are some pros and cons of piece-rate pay:

Employee advantages

- Piece-rate provides a unique opportunity for earning income. Workers who produce quickly can earn more money than people who are paid hourly to do the same work.

- Employees take pride in their productivity because they are responsible from start to finish. They do not need others to help them do their jobs.

- Less supervision is needed because employees know exactly what they need to do to accomplish tasks. Workers make all job related decisions, and they essentially manage themselves.

Employee disadvantages

- Employees who move too quickly can lose focus of quality and end up producing inferior products. They know that slowing down costs them money, so they are willing to sacrifice quality for quantity.

- Piece-rate pay discourages teamwork because employees prefer to work alone in order to earn money for themselves. This prevents people from collaborating with each for new ideas and concepts.

- Piece-rate pay does not help employees build skills outside of speed and productivity. They lack the ability to solve unique problems because their focus is limited.

Merit

This is a traditional type of compensation. Essentially, employee performance is evaluated using an appraisal system, and compensation is adjusted based on the results.

Organizational example

Isabelle is an inventory control manager at a book publisher. She is evaluated by the president of the company once per year, and any increase in her pay is based on that evaluation.

Below are some pros and merit pay:

Employee advantages

- Top performing employees are rewarded for their efforts. They find this motivating because lower performing employees do not receive the same pay increases.

- Merit pay is virtually unlimited in terms of rewards. There is no firmly established "top of the pay scale" because rewards are based on management perception of employees.

- Merit pay is beneficial for people who participate in successful team projects. Members are rewarded for their efforts based on the success of the team.

Employee disadvantages

- Economic conditions can prevent wage increases for employees regardless of their performance. This is demotivating and might cause some workers to stop performing at a high level.

- Equal pay for team members can cause problems because members who did most of the work can become resentful about not being recognized. Management typically rewards the group as a whole rather than recognizing individual members for their achievements.

- Unions typically resist any type of merit pay. Unions are designed for the progression of an entire group rather an individual, and this hurts top performers because they are not rewarded for their efforts.

Skill

This compensation is based on employee expertise rather than more traditional factors such as seniority or specific achievements. Essentially, skill pay is based on worker performance in relation to core competencies such as multi-tasking and leadership.

Organizational example

Jermaine is employed as a general manager in an upscale restaurant. His pay is based on his ability to lead his employees, rather than his accomplishments in areas such as cost savings or profitability.

Below are some pros and cons of skill pay:

Employee advantages

- Seniority has no bearing on compensation. New employees have an opportunity to be well compensated regardless of their experience or years with the organization.

- Employees can focus on their performance as related to specific job attributes. They know they will be rewarded if they do well in certain areas, and they do not have to worry about other unrelated aspects of their jobs.

- Sill based pay promotes self-improvement. Focusing on specific competencies motivates employees to continually improve because they know they are compensated for getting better in those areas.

Employee disadvantages

- Skill based pay can promote a sense of entitlement. Employees who are guaranteed money based on their expertise can become complacent.

- Objectivity is sometimes missing. Evaluation of competencies such as multi-tasking and leadership is very subjective because it is based on personal interpretation.

- Employees can feel unfairly treated if they find out that lesser valued employees received larger monetary increases. This can happen with any type of employee compensation plan, but it is more prevalent with skill based pay due to the subjectivity involved.

Profit sharing

This type of compensation is provided in addition to salary, hourly wages, bonuses, and commissions. It is based on the profitability of the organization, and management determines the amount of the contribution. The money is often paid out when employees leave the organization or retire.

Organizational example

Candice is employed as a stewardess for an airline. She earns a salary and has a benefit package that includes health, dental, and life insurance. Additional compensation for Candice includes a profit sharing retirement plan that the airline contributes to after profitable years.

Below are some pros and cons profit sharing programs:

Employee advantages

- Profit sharing plans are essentially free compensation. Employees have a retirement plan in place without contributing any of their own money.

- Profit sharing plans promote teamwork. Employees work together and focus on making the organization profitable because they share in the rewards.

- Profit sharing plans help employees identify with the organization. Employees feel like they are an active part of the company because their contributions matter.

Employee disadvantages

- Employees have a retirement plan in place that does not consist of their own money, but management determines the amount and time of the contributions. There is also no guarantee that contributions will be made.

- Employees sometimes focus only on profitability... regardless of the consequences. Lower quality or less expensive products might be more profitable in the short-term, but they can have long-term ramifications that negatively impact the organization.

- Profit sharing plans can be demotivating when contributions are not made. People become dependent on these plans for their retirement, and they lose morale when the organization chooses not to contribute.

Gain sharing

Gain sharing is similar to profit sharing with some distinct differences. Both programs are designed for employees to share in the success of organizations. However, contributions to gain sharing programs are not based on profitability. Instead, employees need to meet designated goals in order to receive payouts. Typically these goals involve productivity increases from one period to the next.

Organizational example

Felix is an auto mechanic at a car dealership. He earns an hourly wage and has a benefit package that includes health, dental, and life insurance. Additional compensation for Felix includes a gain sharing plan where management measures the mechanics productivity every quarter and compares it to the previous quarter. If productivity increases, the mechanics receive a payout from the dealership.

Below are some pros and cons of gain sharing programs:

Employee advantages

- Gain sharing is motivational. It inspires employees to increase productivity and improve their financial well-being.

- Gainsharing is paid out regardless of profitability. Employees are paid as long as they reach designated goals.

- Like profit sharing, gain sharing rewards employees for performance. However, gain sharing payments are more frequent because progress is measured and rewarded several times per year.

Employee disadvantages

- Gain sharing motivates employees, but it also has the potential to decrease morale because it is not guaranteed. Employees begin to expect payouts, and they are demotivated when money is not paid out because designated goals were not achieved.

- Gainsharing is not directly based on profitability, but it can disappear if organizations are not profitable. Organizations that are struggling financially need to cut costs, and gain sharing is often one of the first things to go.

- Similar to profit sharing, gain sharing employees sometimes focus only on increasing productivity. When they do this, quality can be lowered to the point where it negatively impacts the organization.

Employee stock ownership

This type of compensation is part of a benefit program where employees can purchase stock. The price of the stock is typically below the market value, and this makes it easier to purchase for workers.

Organizational example

Felicia is a foreman at a gutter and siding company. She is paid a salary and has medical and dental benefits for her family. Felicia also has an opportunity to own part of the company. Every year, her employer offers her the option to buy company stock at 20 percent below the market value. The only stipulation is that this stock cannot be sold until she leaves the company or retires.

Below are some pros and cons of employee stock ownership programs:

Employee advantages

- Employees are interested in the success of the company because they are stock owners. In short, they have a financial interest and want to see it grow.

- Employees tend to become more motivated when they own stock. They want to get involved in ways that help the company grow and prosper because they identify with it through ownership.

- Stock value grows as the organization grows. Employees can accrue large amounts of money as the value of their investment increases. Best of all, they can do this without the stress or headaches of managing the company.

Employee disadvantages

- Stock ownership is not always enough for employees to stay motivated. They also need to be informed of the company status and progress in order to feel involved, and sometimes management fails to address this concern.

- Stock ownership programs are often designated for retirement. If the company performs poorly and the value of the stock decreases, then employees who relied on it for their retirement can end up with little or nothing.

- Often times the stock issued to employees is non-voting in status. This means employees own stock, but they have no voice in the direction of the company.

Benefits

Employee benefits are compensation in addition to an agreed upon wage. They encompass a variety of different components and are based on many factors. However, the major benefits referred to in this section are health insurance, dental insurance, life insurance, vacation, paid days off, and retirement programs.

Organizational example

Quinton just accepted a job as an engineer with an aerospace company. He agreed upon a salary, but the company also offers a benefit package as additional compensation. This package includes health insurance, dental insurance, life insurance, two weeks of paid vacation, three paid days off, and a 401K program with a 25 percent company match.

Below are some pros and cons of benefit packages:

Employee advantages

- Benefit packages often allow employees to make choices, and this is good because people have different needs. They can select the benefits that are most beneficial and pass on the ones that are not essential.

- Good benefit packages are an added incentive to remain with an organization. In fact, benefits are more important than wages for some employees.

- Benefit packages allow employees to monitor and maintain the health of themselves and their families. This is good for the employee and the employer.

Employee disadvantages

- Benefit packages often allow employees to make choices based on their needs, but the wrong choice can create financial problems. Quite simply, it is hard for employees to know what benefits will be needed in the future.

- Good benefit packages can force employees to stay at jobs that they dislike. They might want to move on to something that pays a higher wage or is more interesting, but they cannot make a change because they need the benefits offered by their current employer.

- The costs of benefits are constantly rising for organizations, and they need to pass some of this on to the employees. This means employees are required to pay for their benefits, and some opt out if they cannot afford to do so. When this happens, the benefits offered by the organization are no longer beneficial to the employee.

Work-life balance

Work-life balance involves accomplishing work related goals while enjoying life outside of work. As people's lives become busier and more hectic, they begin to realize the importance of work-life balance. Time is limited, and different things need to take priority at different times in life. People need to work in order to sustain a certain lifestyle, but they also need the time to enjoy that lifestyle.

Organizational example

Jaquelin works as a pediatric nurse at a hospital. The hospital has a work-life balance program in place where trained counselors are available to listen to the problems the hospital employees are experiencing at home or at work. This program provides employees with someone who acts as a sounding board and offers advice when needed...and it helps Jaquelin cope with the stress of her job.

Below are some pros and cons or work-life balance programs:

Employee advantages

- Stress is reduced. Work-life balance programs such as counseling and therapy help relieve stress and prevent the consequences that result from it.

- Physical health is improved. Gym memberships and exercise areas help employees maintain physical health at work and at home.

- Telecommuting is a huge benefit for many employees. They can perform their job from home and not have to worry about traffic or restrictive work schedules.

Employee disadvantages

- Career progression is hampered. Telecommuters who are not involved in the day-to-day activities of the organization can be passed up by others simply because they are not physically noticed. This is a major concern for employees who whose jobs are completely remote.

- Telecommuting can cause communication issues. Typically the major form of communication for employees working remotely is the written word (email, text, letter)...and written words can easily be misinterpreted.

- Cost is a concern. Expenses can force organizations to eliminate work-life balance programs, and the loss of these programs can be demotivating to the employees who found them useful.

Now you have an understanding of the basic types of pay and compensation available for employees. Leaders in organizations need to figure out which types work best for their workforces in order to keep people content and productive. Ultimately, this requires finding and maintaining a balance between satisfied workers and a financially stable organization.

Summary

Compensation is very important to employees. It affects their motivation and commitment, and it is a major factor in determining their longevity with organizations. People want to find happiness at work, and compensation always seems to factor into that happiness.

This book focuses on employee pay and compensation in organizations. It examines various types of pay structures and benefits including salary pay, hourly pay, commission based pay, bonus pay, piece-rate pay, merit pay, skill pay, profit sharing programs, gain sharing programs, employee stock ownership programs, work-life balance programs, and benefit packages. Each type of compensation is described, discussed in terms of pros and cons, and illustrated using a workplace example.

Congratulations! You know have a better understanding of employee pay and compensation...two importance aspects of people's jobs that affect their organizational behavior.

Employee Reviews
The Appraisal Process and Methods for Improvement

Louis Bevoc

Published by
NutriNiche System LLC

Louis Bevoc books...simple explanations of complex subjects

Introduction — 35
Types — 35
- Supervisor — 35
- Self — 36
- Peer — 37
- 360 — 37
- MBO — 38
- Scale — 38

Challenges — 39
- Supervisor — 39
- Self — 40
- Peer — 40
- 360 — 40
- MBO — 41
- Scale — 41

Improving — 42
- Supervisor — 42
- Self — 43
- Peer — 44
- 360 — 45
- MBO — 45
- Scale — 46

Summary — 46

Introduction

Leaders of organizations must be able to determine if employees are meeting workplace expectations, and this is best done by using some type of review system that measures their performance. Performance involves standards, levels, or grades that need to be met or exceeded for a particular job or position. Sometimes this can be quantified, like reaching certain numbers for sales or production, but other times it is a bit more complex. For example, it's hard to quantify requirements for research scientists because they typically do not have quotas that need to be achieved. Performance for these individuals might best be measured by the progress and application of their studies and findings.

Without reviews, employees would be somewhat lost. They would not know if they are meeting workplace expectations, and they would find it difficult to achieve organizational goals and objectives. The review process indicates good standing of employees and allows them to monitor their progress as they grow within the organization. Once reviews are complete, employee strengths and weaknesses can be determined and plans for improvement can be implemented if necessary.

This book focuses on specific types of employee reviews, the challenges involved with them, and the best ways for improving them. The types of reviews discussed include *Supervisor, Self, Peer, 360, MBO,* and *Scale*. Each type is analyzed and applied to organizations using workplace examples for better understanding.

Let's begin by discussing the various types of reviews that are used in organizations.

Types

Employee reviews need to be categorized for a better understanding of their importance in the workplace. The following are specific types of reviews that occur in organizations:

Supervisor

This type of review typically involves a one-on-one encounter with the supervisor and employee. The supervisor completes a written evaluation with questions related to performance, including strengths and weaknesses, and discusses it with the employee. The employee has the right to challenge any of aspect of the supervisor's evaluation, and disputes that cannot be resolved are taken to a higher level of management. Once the review is agreed upon by both parties, it becomes a permanent part of the employee's file.

The major advantage of the supervisor review is efficiency. Supervisors typically understand the job responsibilities and expectations of their subordinates. Their familiarity allows them to easily answer most of the review questions, and they are able to make a fairly accurate assessment of employee performance in a reasonable amount of time.

Organizational example

Scott is the production manager in a juice manufacturing plant. He reports to the plant manager Jennifer, and today is his annual review.

Jennifer understands Scott's job responsibilities well because she was the production manager prior to being promoted to plant manager. She thinks he does a good job professionally and also likes him personally. Scott also just finished a project for her that was very successful.

Jennifer answers the review questions on the designated form with no difficulty and then meets with Scott to discuss the details of her evaluation. Scott believes the review is fair and accurate, and it becomes a part of his permanent employee file. This review is simple to conduct and takes less than one hour to complete.

In short, Jennifer understands Scott's job quite well and likes him on a personal and professional level. This allows her to accurately appraise him in a short period of time.

Self

Self-reviews involve employees rating themselves on pre-designated criteria established by the organization. Employees identify their strengths and weaknesses in a variety of areas including performance and work relationships, and they suggest areas where they can improve and grow professionally.

This evaluation can be done using essay responses or a Likert scale. Essays provide a detailed account of employee perceptions, while Likert scales have a range, for instance from 1 to 5, that gives a quantifiable score.

An advantage of self-reviews is that employees gain awareness of their actions and their relationships with others, and this leads to increased accountability.

Organizational example

Ralph works as a bar tender at a restaurant that is part of a national chain. He has his six-month review scheduled for today, and corporate management has just informed him that he needs to do a self-evaluation for this appraisal.

Ralph evaluates himself using a Likert scale provided by the company. He rates himself between 1 (poor) and 10 (excellent) for the 20 different categories that assess his performance, growth, and work relationships.

Ralph's scores indicate he has a good relationship with his immediate supervisor, but he needs to improve in three different areas. Because he found the areas for improvement on his own, he is motivated to take accountability and make the necessary changes. These changes should come fairly easy due to the positive association he has with his manager.

Peer

Peer reviews are conducted by team members or coworkers, rather than by the employees themselves or their supervisors. Specifically, peers are asked to anonymously rate the performance of their coworkers. These comments are usually given the supervisor of the employee being reviewed, but sometimes they are also shared directly with the employee.

An advantage of peer reviews is that they are often perceived as more fair than reviews conducted by a supervisor because multiple minds provide a more accurate judgment of performance. Additionally, peer reviews are valuable to the workplace in general because they create a culture that encourages feedback and teamwork.

Organizational example

William works as a teller at a bank. His review is scheduled for today, and it will be conducted by his peers. Seven other tellers have shared their opinions about William's performance with Joan, the bank manager.

Joan gathers the information and finds that William is well liked by employees and customers, but he has trouble arriving at work on time. Joan was not aware of this because William starts earlier than her, but she makes sure she shares this information with him.

William is happy that others perceive him as an excellent customer service person. However, he also realizes that his tardiness is an issue because everyone sees it as an area where he needs to improve. Based on his coworkers' analysis, William begins to leave his home earlier in the morning to make sure he arrives to work on time.

In summary, William perceived his peers' critique as fair and legitimate because other tellers had similar comments regarding his performance.

360

This review uses self-analysis, peer assessment, supervisor feedback, and subordinate evaluation (if applicable) for the appraisal. It assesses self-perception (from employees being reviewed), performance (from supervisors), character (from peers), and leadership skills (from subordinates).

The major advantage of the 360 review is that it gives a complete picture of employee performance based on input from multiple sources.

Organizational example

Wanda is a supervisor at an automotive supplier. Her review is today, and her company has decided to a 360 appraisal. The Human resources manager meets with Wanda, her boss, three other supervisors, and three of her direct reports. The appraisal process takes place over the next three days, and the various evaluations do a wonderful job portraying Wanda's performance. Without the input of these different employees, the review would not have as detailed or complete.

In short, Wanda's job performance was clearly depicted due to the diversity of the employees who participated in her evaluation

MBO

MBO is an acronym for "Management By Objectives" that was first popularized in 1954 by management guru Peter Drucker. It involves employees and supervisors working together to establish goals that need to be achieved in a certain time frame. The thinking behind this type of appraisal is that employees who are involved in setting their own goals will be more motivated to accomplish them.

The advantage of MBO reviews is that it is easy to establish success or failure at the next review. Employees are successful if the goals have been achieved, and they have failed if the goals have not been achieved.

Organizational example

Katrina is a sales representative for a line of cosmetics, and her boss Patrick decides to do an MBO evaluation at her mid-year review. Patrick asks Katrina what goals she would like to set for herself. She knows she needs to sell $400,000 worth of product to get a bonus, but she wants to do better. She sets a goal of $500,000 in sales, and Patrick agrees.

For the next six months, Katrina works very hard. She wants to achieve her goal because she established it, and this makes her feel more personally involved. At her year-end review, she achieves her goal of $500,000 in sales, and Patrick rewards her with a raise in her base pay.

In summary, Katrina's involvement in setting a work related goal during her mid-year review motivated her to achieve that goal. By her year-end review, she achieved the goal she established for herself, and Patrick rewarded her for being successful.

Scale

This is a less popular type of review than most of the others because the management has to speed time and effort developing the questions and rating scale that will be used. Essentially, it is a grading system that assesses a variety of aspects related to employee performance including job skills, communication, collaboration, and understanding. Employees need to meet a minimum score, similar to that in education, in order for their review to be considered successful. Those who do not meet the minimum score are put on a performance improvement plan.

The advantage of scale reviews is they are custom made for organizations. This gives management the ability to ask questions that are specific to a particular workplace.

Organizational example

John is a salesperson at a mortgage company, and his review is being conducted using the scale method. John has sold the second most mortgages in the company, proving that he understands his job and is productive. He is also well liked by employees and customers and works well with others on team projects. John easily meets the minimum performance score, and this means that he is successful as a salesperson.

John's job skills, communication, collaboration, and understanding help him achieve a very good score in his review, and this indicates that he is competent in his position.

You now understand some specific types of reviews and the benefits they provide. However, those benefits are sometimes overshadowed by the limitations involved, and that is why the next section is dedicated to the challenges facing the various appraisal processes.

Challenges

As noted above, reviews provide a lot of useful information for employees and managers. However, they are not without challenges, and some of those challenges are discussed in this section.

To make these challenges easier to understand, the same examples from the *Types* section will be used for this section. This time, however, they will be changed to show how the review being discussed has limitations.

Please consider the following:

Supervisor

Supervisor reviews are efficient because bosses typically understand their subordinates job responsibilities and expectations. However, problems with the type of appraisal do exist, and they revolve around bias or slanted thinking.

One issue is the fact these reviews are subjective. A yearly review by a supervisor might be based on the employee's most recent performance, and that performance might not accurately reflect the entire year.

Another concern is the reviews are based on the opinion of one individual. That opinion might not be accurate, and it typically goes unchallenged by anyone else with the authority to make a judgment.

In both situations, the appraisal is not only unfair to the employee being evaluated, it is also unjust for the organizational because they are receiving inaccurate information.

Organizational example

In the *Types* section example, Jenny liked Scott personally and professionally, and this made the review easy for her. However, Scott just finished a big project that was very successful, and that success was in Jenny's recent memory. It caused her to forget about the performance issues Scott experienced at the beginning of the year.

In reality, Jenny's review was unjust to Scott and the juice manufacturer because the documented information was not entirely accurate.

Self

Self-evaluations help employees become aware of the areas they need to improve and motivate them to be accountable. However, this only works if employees are honest with their evaluation….and this is not always the case. For instance, employees might avoid negative supervisor ratings for fear of retaliation or some other undesired outcome.

Organizational example

In the *Types* section example, Ralph evaluated himself and determined that he had a great working relationship with his supervisor. This relationship, however, may be good because his boss is very easy on him. Ralph might be able to do whatever he wants at work with little supervisor intervention, and he does not want this to change based on a critical rating.

Peer

Peer reviews are often perceived as fair because they are conducted by more than one person. This provides a more accurate judgment of the employee being evaluated because more people's opinions are involved. However, a disadvantage of this type of review is peers tend to evaluate coworkers from a personal, rather than professional, level. If they don't like the person, it will reflect their rating in a negative manner.

Organizational example

In the *Types* section example, William found his peers' critiques helpful and legitimate. However, William is well like by the other tellers. If they did not like him, this would stand in the way of a positive evaluation…regardless of the fact he works well with customers. The end result would be an inaccurate evaluation that casts a negative light on William.

360

The 360 review is very comprehensive because it involves the viewpoints of many different people. However, meeting with all these people is expensive and time consuming. It requires money and time that some organizations simply do not have.

Organizational example

In the *Types* section example, Wanda's appraisal was detailed and complete due to the variety of people involved. However, it required taking seven people away from their jobs for interviews, and it took three days to complete. In short, the 360 review requires valuable resources that many organizations cannot or will not sacrifice.

MBO

The major advantage of MBO reviews is that it is easy to determine success or failure at the next review. Employees are successful if the established goals have been achieved, and they have failed if the established goals have not been achieved. However, employees who fail might lose the motivation and desire to try again…and this is bad for employees and organizations.

Organizational example

In the *Types* section example, Katrina set a goal at her mid-year review and achieved it by her year-end review. Because she was successful, she was rewarded with a raise in her base pay.

If Katrina had not met her goal, her year-end review would have been considerably different. She would not have received the raise, and she would be demotivated by her lack of success. The organization would also suffer because Katrina's failure might deter her from trying again, and she might start looking for other employment.

Scale

Scale reviews are custom made so they allow management the ability to ask questions regarding job skills, communication, collaboration, and understanding that are specific to a particular workplace. However, certain questions can work against introverted individuals. Some people choose their career because it allows them to work independently. They prefer not to socialize or collaborate and typically do not need to do so during their daily activities.

Organizational example

In the *Types* section example, John proved to be competent in his position as a salesperson. He easily met the minimum performance score because he was productive and worked well with others.

The scale review, however, does not give a fair evaluation of other employees at the mortgage company. Marlene is an accountant who rarely needs to interact with people. She is very good at her job, and most of her communication can be done using email. She is an introvert, prefers to work alone, and chose her career based on her work preferences.

Marlene might not achieve the minimum score to be considered successful using the scale system. She is very competent in her position, but her communication and collaboration rating might indicate otherwise. If this is the case, she would need to follow a performance improvement plan, and that would be demotivating for her.

Regardless of the challenges involved with appraisals, they are a necessary part of organizations and will continue to be used until something better comes along. That being said, there need to be ways to make them better...and that is the focus of the next section.

Improving

Since there are obvious challenges involved with reviews, it makes sense that they should try to be improved upon. This section examines ways to make reviews better.

To make these methods simpler to comprehend, we will use the same examples from the *Types and Challenges* sections. This time, however, they will be modified to show how the review being discussed can be improved.

Please consider the following:

Supervisor

Supervisor reviews have an advantage of being efficient because bosses are familiar with their subordinate's job responsibilities, and they can make an assessment in a relatively short period of time. However, these reviews are very subjective and can be biased. Additionally, they might be based on the most recent performance of employees, rather than the entire time period for which they are being reviewed.

Ways to improve supervisor reviews include:

Implement training

Supervisors need to be properly trained in order to give meaningful reviews. This training will teach them how to provide positive and negative feedback in a way that helps employees become successful and achieve organizational objectives. This is best done in face-to-face meetings, but web-based resources and tools can be provided for reference at any time.

Monitor appraisals

Supervisor appraisals need to be monitored after they are completed due to the subjectivity and potential bias involved. This is best done by someone in upper management who makes sure the evaluation is accurate and the employee and organization are being treated fairly.

Utilize other supervisors

Supervisors should meet with each to discuss the review process. This collaboration encourages learning, promotes best practices, and creates consistency of appraisals throughout the organization.

Organizational example

In the *Types* and *Challenges* section example, Scott just finished a big project that was very successful, and that success caused Jenny to forget about the performance issues he had at the beginning of the year. Due to this, her review of him was inaccurate.

The inaccuracy in this review could have been avoided if Jenny was properly trained. She could have been taught how to reflect on the entire year and provide difficult feedback to help Scott improve in the areas that he is weak.

Additionally, Jenny's appraisal should have been reviewed by someone in higher management. This monitoring would have discovered that Jenny did not note any negative aspects of Scott's performance. She could then have been instructed to go through training in order to perform reviews that are best for the employee and the company.

Self

The advantage of self-reviews is that employees gain awareness by identifying their strengths and weaknesses, and this leads to increased accountability. However, this evaluation only works if the employees are truthful about their perceptions. Dishonestly is common during self-appraisals due to fear of retaliation and other negative outcomes.

The best way to improve self-reviews is to get upper management involved. They can hold meetings to encourage truthful and meaningful thinking that promotes accurate self-evaluations. Specifically, the goals of these meetings are to:

Encourage self-promotion

Employees who believe they are doing well in certain areas need to be able to express this without being thought of as bragging. Accomplishments and successes must be noted for recognition and rewards, and this starts with the persuasion of upper management.

Encourage constructive criticism

Employees who have negative feelings about supervisors must be able to express them without fear of those supervisors retaliating. The best protection from this retaliation comes from managers at the top, and they need to communicate their intent to supervisors and employees.

Encourage objectivity

Employees who know they need to improve in certain areas must realize their weaknesses and seek to get better. Employees who are not objective risk losing an opportunity to grow and progress within the organization...and leadership needs to make this clear.

Encourage requests for guidance

Employees who face challenges must feel comfortable asking for help in the form of training, teaching, or mentoring. They also need to know that they will receive assistance when they ask for it, and upper management can provide that assistance.

Encourage planning

Employees need confidence to plan for their future. They need to know where they are and where they want to go, and this is made possible with the support of organizational leadership.

In short, improvement of self-reviews stems from top management guiding employees, holding them accountable, protecting them, and making them aware that self-appraisals are part of a learning process that benefits their professional growth.

Organizational example

In the *Types* and *Challenges* section example, Ralph was objective in his self-review because he found areas where he needed to improve. He also determined that he had a good working relationship with his supervisor, but this might have been because his boss was very easy on him.

If Ralph is doing whatever he wants to do with little supervision, then he is not progressing or learning...and this could have been pointed out to him by company leaders. Meetings with management could have made it clear that he needed to find some constructive criticism about his boss for the review to be truly beneficial.

Peer

The advantage of peer reviews is that they are perceived as fair by employees because the evaluation comes from several people rather than one supervisor. However, peers tend to evaluate each other based on personal, rather than professional, relationships.

Personal relationships at work are important, but they do not accurately represent job performance. Some employees are very good at their jobs, but they are not well liked by others. Other employees are well liked by coworkers, but they are not very good at their jobs.

Since peer reviews are often based on personal relationships, the best way to improve them is to avoid using them for monetary compensation, promotions, or disciplinary action. Instead, they should be used as reference tools to help upper management make decisions related to these three areas.

Organizational example

In the *Types* and *Challenges* section example, William was well liked by others. Due to this, he was rated as an excellent customer service person. If he was not well liked, his rating likely would have been much lower. In either case, the rating would be somewhat inaccurate because it is based on personal likes and dislikes rather than performance.

Although Williams review was based mostly on personal relationships, it did have value. It made him realize that he needs to get to work earlier to avoid being late. It also encouraged collaboration among his peers, and this helps improve the overall communication at the bank.

Williams rating, however, should not be used to determine his pay, bonus, or potential for promotion. It should be used by bank executives, along with other tools such as his supervisor's review, to establish these important job aspects.

360

The 360 review is advantageous because it uses multiple sources (self, coworkers, higher management, and subordinates) at a variety of hierarchy levels for the evaluation. However, this appraisal is also time consuming and costly, so it is not feasible for some organizations.

Planning and commitment are important for improving the 360 review. Planning involves making sure the proper resources, time and money, are available from start to finish. Top management also needs to be committed to being part of the process, rather than spectators on the sidelines.

Organizational example

In the *Types* and *Challenges* section example, Wanda's review involved seven people and took three days to complete. Her appraisal was detailed and complete, but three days is a long time for an evaluation. Better planning should have been made in advance to make sure the employees being interviewed for the assessment were ready at the designated times. This would have saved time that could have been better used in those employees' daily jobs. Additionally, a person in an executive position at the automotive supplier should have been present during the interviews. Although this might seem like additional resources being utilized, executives see important areas of evaluations that need to be addressed, and they help expedite the overall process.

MBO

The advantage of MBO reviews is they make it simple to establish success and failure. If objectives have been achieved, then the employee is successful. If objectives have not been achieved, then the employee has failed.

A clear distinction between success and failure is good for those who succeed, but it is not good for those who fail. In fact, those who fail might not be motivated to try again, and this is bad for the employee and the organization.

MBO appraisals can be improved by providing adequate time and training. Employees and supervisors need to be properly trained in order to understand how to set realistic objectives that are achievable...and this takes time.

Organizational example

In the *Types* and *Challenges* section example, Katrina was successful because she accomplished her objectives. However, she might not be successful in her next review, and this could discourage her from trying again. If Katrina undergoes training on how to set realistic objectives, then she could avoid the failure of not reaching her objectives. This requires time, but the payback will be worth it because Katrina's continual success is important for helping the company thrive and prosper. In other words, Katrina's success is directly related to the success of the organization.

Scale

Scale reviews have an advantage over other types of evaluations because organizations can design them to fit specific needs. However, these appraisals are not good for employees who are introverted or work independently.

Scale reviews can be improved by eliminating or modifying some of the questions that evaluate communication and collaboration for certain individuals. In other words, the evaluation will change based on the personality and/or position of the employee.

Organizational example

In the *Types* and *Challenges* section example, John did quite well on the scale appraisal because he is an extroverted salesperson. The same review, however, is not fair to Marlene because she is an introverted accountant. Management needs to take this discrepancy into account and alter some of the communication and collaboration questions for Marlene so she gets an accurate review and avoids being put on a demotivating performance improvement plan.

Summary

Employee reviews are an important aspect of most organizations because they evaluate an individual's performance. They indicate a worker's strengths and weaknesses, and they play a large role in determining that person's monetary compensation and promotion opportunities. Without reviews, employees would not know if they are progressing at their jobs, and they would not understand their job expectations.

This book uses thoughtful analysis and workplace examples to examine specific types of employee reviews, the challenges involved with them, and the best ways for improving them. The types of reviews discussed include *Supervisor, Self, Peer, 360, MBO,* and *Scale.*

After reading the material in this book, you will have a better understanding of reviews and their importance in the workplace.

Absenteeism in Organizations
Causes, Effects, and Prevention

Louis Bevoc

Published by
NutriNiche System LLC

Louis Bevoc books...simple explanations of complex subjects

Introduction 51
Causes 51
- Stress 52
- Family care 52
- Bereavement 53
- Illness 53
- Bullying 54
- Poor supervision 54
- Workload 54
- Working conditions 54
- Travel 55
- Personal reasons 55
- Injury 55
- Other employment 56
- Job searches 56
- Transportation 56
- Excessive hours 56
- Strange hours 56
- Religion 56
- Drugs and alcohol 57
- Attitude 57
- Age 57
- Seniority 57
- Boredom 57
- Family Businesses 58
- Unrecognized holidays 58
- Homeland visits 58

Effects 58
- Costs 58
- Productivity 59
- Morale 59
- Trust 59
- Stress 59
- Turnover 60

Prevention 60
- Hiring practices 60

Rewards 61
　　　Job rotation 61
　　　Communication 62
Summary 62

Introduction

Absenteeism is employees' unscheduled absence from their jobs. The key word here is "unscheduled." Scheduled absences can be planned for in advance, and this helps avoid some of the potential problems that might occur during the employees' time off. However, there is very little time to plan for unscheduled absences, and the necessary resources might not be available at a moment's notice.

Leaders in organizations are not naive enough to think employees are going to be at work on every scheduled day. They expect workers to miss some time because they are not feeling well or want to attend to personal matters that conflict with the times they are supposed to be at work. This is acceptable and does not present a problem...unless it becomes excessive.

When absenteeism becomes excessive, it is a major headache for organizations. If employees do not show up for work, then their jobs need to be performed by someone else. If no one else is available, then those jobs simply do not get done. This creates difficult and stressful situations for workers and managers, and it occurs far too often in some workplaces.

Absenteeism has a greater impact on smaller organizations than it does on larger ones due to the size of the workforces. For example, a business with 100 employees will function close to normal if five people are absent. However, a business with eight employees might operate if five workers are missing.

Regardless of the number of employees in a workplace, excessive absenteeism causes problems. It stresses out the employees who are forced to take on additional workloads, lowers morale, and affects productivity. Ultimately, it impacts the financial well-being of organizations as they struggle to meet the needs of their customers.

Since there are problems associated with absenteeism, leaders of organizations need to do whatever they can to minimize it. This starts by gaining a better understanding of the causes and effects.

This eBook examines the causes and effects of absenteeism. It explores the reasons employees miss scheduled days of work and analyzes the problems this causes for organizations. It also offers suggestions for preventing workplace absenteeism so the negative effects can be minimized.

Now that you have a basic understanding of workplace absenteeism and the scope of this eBook, let's move on to discussing the causes of this problem.

Causes

As noted in the introduction, absenteeism is employees' unscheduled absence from their jobs. Unscheduled absence can be intentional or unintentional as shown in the following examples:

Intentional absenteeism

Manny comes home from work on Wednesday night and finds an envelope in his front door. As a surprise, one of his best friends leaves two baseball tickets to the Atlanta Braves home opening game that starts Thursday at noon. Manny is thrilled, and he texts his friend that he will be at the game.

The next morning, Manny calls his employer and tells them that he will not be in to work. He says he has some "personal business" that he needs to attend to, and he will return on Friday.

Manny's decision to miss work in order to go to the baseball game is an example of intentional absenteeism.

Unintentional absenteeism

Juanita and George are married with two children under the age of five. They both work full time jobs, and her husband frequently travels. This week he is away on a business trip.

George's business trips are normally not a problem for Juanita because drops her children off at day care in the morning before going into work. However, this morning she wakes up to find her daughter vomiting. This child will not be able to go to day care today and Juanita is the only person who can care for her. She calls work and tells them that she will not be in today due to a sick child.

Juanita's decision to miss work in order to take care of a sick child is an example unintentional absenteeism.

In the view of an employer, Juanita's decision is much more legitimate than Manny's for missing work. However, regardless of the intent, unscheduled absences do not allow organizations to plan for handling missing employee's work that needs to be completed. For this reason, it is important to understand the causes of absenteeism so attempts can be made to eliminate them and minimize absences on scheduled work days.

It is virtually impossible to list every cause of absenteeism due to the fact that every employee is unique. However, the following are some major causes of these unscheduled absences:

Stress

Work related stress can lead to mental and physical health problems if it is not dealt with in some manner. Employees use a variety of different techniques to deal with stress including yoga, exercise, meditation, relaxation, massage, and therapy. However, workers also deal with stress by not showing up for work...and this is why it is a cause of absenteeism.

Family care

Family care has changed considerably since the 1960s. Mothers used to stay home to take care of children while fathers worked to financially support the family. However, this has changed. Today many, if not most mothers, are employed in some capacity. Children go to day care and are picked up after the parent's workdays are finished.

The dual income family works well financially for many families, but this arrangement poses a problem when children get sick. One of the parents needs to stay home to care for the child, and this means that he or she needs to miss work. Although this absence is unintentional, it is still unscheduled and therefore classified as absenteeism.

Family care absenteeism does not end with care for children. Employees today are part of the "sandwich generation" where they need to help young children and aging parents. When a parent needs assistance, one of their children needs to miss work to provide the necessary care...and the end result is an unscheduled absence. So, the same people who miss work for their children can also miss work for their parents.

In short, family care today is a major cause of absenteeism based on dual income households and the needs of various relatives. This will continue to present a challenge as long as working couples have young children and aging parents.

Bereavement

An old saying goes, "two things people have to do during life are die and pay taxes." The taxes part is debatable...but the part about dying is an absolute fact.

When people die, friends and family need time to grieve over the loss. However, it is difficult to specify how long employees should mourn because everyone is different. Some workers need more time than others and therefore end up missing more days of work. Since this missed time is unscheduled, it is considered absenteeism.

Illness

Essentially, illness can be physical or mental. Physical illness can be as simple as the common cold or as serious as terminal cancer. Mental illness often involves some type of depression, but it can also involve issues such as paranoia or schizophrenia.

The following examines the two types of illness in more detail:

> Physical illness
>
> It is not uncommon for employees to become physically ill. Their illnesses often require them to miss work, and the number of days they are absent depends on the time required for healing.
>
> Management expects employees to miss some time at work due to physical illness, but that time is not scheduled in advance and is therefore deemed absenteeism.
>
> *Mental illness*
>
> Mental illness is not as common as physical illness, but it does affect employees in every type of workplace. This illness often requires people to miss work, and they are not able to return until their conditions are cured or controlled.

Management typically does not expect employees to miss work due to mental illness, but they do understand that it does occur. However, the time missed is unscheduled and is therefore considered absenteeism.

Bullying

Employees who are bullied by coworkers might choose to stay home rather than come to work and take the abuse. This type of situation is unfortunate because bullying can lead to depression and long-term negative effects. Bullying might not be one of the most common causes of absenteeism, but it is one of the most important due to other problems that can result.

Poor supervision

Poor supervision is a problem in many organizations, but only the more severe cases result in absenteeism. Employees simply cannot bear to see their supervisors, so they decide to call in sick. They become overwhelmed with negative thoughts and choose to avoid the situation rather than deal with bosses that they disdain.

Workload

Workloads can be so excessive that employees choose to stay home rather than go to work. Ironically, the absenteeism resulting from workloads is often an indirect consequence of other absenteeism. This is because employees miss work and their coworkers have to do their jobs. Those coworkers then have much larger workloads, so they also decide to not show up for work. Unfortunately, this cycle can repeat itself until the overworked employees burn out and permanently leave the organization.

Working conditions

Working conditions have a big impact on absenteeism. Workplace temperature, sanitary conditions, and ergonomics all play role in determining if employees will show up for work. Please consider the following examples:

Cold temperatures (workplace temperature)

Cold temperatures create discomfort and cause workers to lose focus. All they think about is getting to a warmer environment, and that in itself is enough to make them not show up for work.

Dirty workplaces (sanitary conditions)

Unsanitary conditions result in mental disgust for some employees. They would rather be home than in a dirty workplace and decide not to come to work.

Poor lighting (ergonomics)

Dimly lit areas cause eye strain. This makes it difficult to complete work and causes headaches. Due to the pain, employees call in sick.

Travel

Some jobs require employees to travel. This is not a problem unless the travel becomes excessive. Employees do not want to constantly be on the road because they miss out on many aspects of their personal lives. When they finally get home, they want to spend time with family and friends rather than going right into the office…so they tell their employer that they will not be in. This is understandable, even in the eyes of some employers, but it is still considered absenteeism.

Personal reasons

There are times when people do not go to work for personal reasons. They choose to attend a daytime sporting event, catch a matinee movie, go on a day trip with a friend, or just relax in front of the television at home. This is also known as "playing hooky," and it happens in workplaces all over the world.

Employers typically do not view personal reasons as legitimate excuses for missing work. However, they realize that employees are going to "play hooky," and there is not much that can be done about it. This form of absenteeism will likely occur in some capacity as long as people work for organizations.

Injury

Injuries are legitimate reasons for missing work. When employees are hurt, they cannot perform certain aspects of their jobs, and therefore need to be off work.

As far as employers are concerned, there two basic types of injuries including:

Work related

These injuries result from accidents that occur on the job. Workers' compensation pays for the employees' time missed because the injury occurred while working. This is bad for the employer for two different reasons because (1) their insurance premiums increase due to the claims and (2) their employees are not able to perform their jobs.

Non-work related

These injuries result from accidents that do not occur on the job. Employers are not required by law to compensate employees who are not injured at work…although some provide short-term and long-term disability benefits. Employers save money by not paying injured employees, but they still lose because these individuals are not able to perform their jobs.

Employers realize that injuries are going to occur. However, these claims can be abused. Workers who do not want to come back to work can often get doctors to extend their excused absence regardless of whether or not they are healed. If this happens, then absenteeism is even more costly to employers...especially if workers compensation is being paid to the injured employees.

Other employment

Some employees miss work because they are working other jobs. This is usually not acceptable to employers...and some even consider it grounds for termination. However, regardless of the rules in place, other employment is a cause of absenteeism that occurs in many workplaces.

Job searches

This involves missing work to (1) look for another job or (2) interview at another organization. Obviously, most employers would frown upon this because they are on the verge of losing employees...and those employees might be going to competitors. However, in reality, missing work for job searching is fairly common because interviews are typically conducted during normal working hours.

Transportation

Most people need some type of transportation to get to their jobs. If that transportation is not available, then they are unable to show up for work. This type of problem is more common for employees who rely on public transportation, but personal vehicles also break down.

Transportation issues are usually beyond the control of employees. However, they are still considered unscheduled absences and a cause of absenteeism.

Excessive hours

Employees who work too many hours sometimes miss work just to get some personal time away from the job. For example, a production plant might be working seven days a week. After two or three weeks without a day off, employees decide to stay home and rest instead of going into work. This rest is obviously justified, but it is considered absenteeism.

Strange hours

Some employees miss work because they work strange shifts or hours. For example, third shift employees might never get to see their families or friends, so they decide to not come into work in order to attend special events in their lives. This type of absenteeism it is more likely to happen to employees who work when most people are at home or out socializing.

Religion

Leaders in organizations are beginning to realize that employees need time off for designated religious occasions that might not be recognized by the government. However, this type of management thinking is in its infancy, and it will be a while before employees are excused for the days they consider sacred. Until that time, workers will not show up for work for religious reasons, and their unscheduled absences will be considered absenteeism.

Drugs and alcohol

Substance abuse is an issue in many workplaces, and this is likely to continue as long as drugs and alcohol are readily available to employees. In some cases, management is required by law to allow employees time to deal with their addictions…and these absences are not part of absenteeism since they are scheduled. However, hangovers and other substance related aftermath are considered absenteeism, and they will likely never be accepted as legitimate by leaders of organizations.

Attitude

Attitude is a major cause of absenteeism. Employees who have negative attitudes about their place of work tend to show up less frequently than coworkers with positive attitudes. Attitude is about perception…and perception truly is reality.

Age

Age is also a cause of absenteeism. Typically, younger workers miss time because they are out socializing or having fun. Older employees often miss time for health concerns or family situations.

Younger and older employees miss work for different reasons, but all of those reasons result in unscheduled absences.

Seniority

Long-term employees sometimes feel a sense of entitlement when in terms of taking unscheduled time off from work. They have been with the organization for a long time and believe their seniority gives them the right to be absent without notice. Unfortunately, this is still considered absenteeism…and it requires other employees to do extra work.

Boredom

Repetition makes jobs mundane. Employees lose the motivation to work after repeating the same task throughout their work day, and this leads them to take unscheduled days off work. In short, boredom is a cause of absenteeism because it does not provide employees with challenges.

Some causes of absenteeism are specific to certain groups of employees such as immigrants. These include:

Family businesses

Some employees miss work because they need to work at seasonal family businesses. For example, they might need to leave to help their family work the fields during harvesting periods.

Absenteeism caused by family businesses can be a big problem for organizations if too many workers leave at the same time. Mass exodus of employees can cripple productivity and even force some organizations to cease operations.

Unrecognized holidays

Similar to religious occasions, some holidays are not recognized by organizations in the United States. Examples include Cinco de Mayo, Greek Easter, and Rosh Hashanah.

Management is beginning to realize that employees need time off for designated holidays, but it will be a while before they are formally excused. Until that time, workers will not show up for work on days they consider holidays, and their unscheduled absences will be considered absenteeism.

Homeland visits

Some employees miss work because they go back to their homelands to visit friends and family. These visits are very important to these workers, and they leave regardless of whether their absences are approved by management.

This type of absenteeism is difficult to prevent because employees have strong ties to people from their countries of origin.

Now you understand some of the major causes of absenteeism, and this is important in order to develop methods of prevention. However, before exploring ways to prevent absenteeism, the effects that it has on workplaces needs to be examined.

Effects

Absenteeism negatively affects employers and employees in a variety of different ways. Some of the major ways include:

Costs

There are high costs associated with absenteeism. Some of these costs are:

Wages and benefits

In many cases, especially those involving worker's compensation, absent employees still receive wages and benefits until they are able to return to work. In some cases, these payouts can go on for years...and possibly even the rest of the employees' lives.

Overtime

As noted earlier, absent employees leave work behind that still needs to be done by coworkers. Those coworkers need to work longer hours to complete the designated tasks, and they are paid overtime for those hours.

Training

Absent workers sometimes need to be replaced by new employees. These new employees need to be trained...and that training has a cost associated with it.

Administrative

Many people are not aware that there are administrative costs for managing absenteeism. For short-term absences, letters need to be sent to the offenders detailing disciplinary action. For long-term absences such as those involving workers' compensation, massive amounts of paperwork need to be filled out...and this takes time and resources. Additionally, meetings need to be conducted with insurance companies, medical providers, and attorneys to discuss the specifics of the case.

In short, absenteeism impacts the bottom lines of organizations. This impact is never good, and it can lead to some companies permanently shutting down.

Productivity

Absenteeism results in decreased productivity. This is due to the fact that experienced employees are missing from the workplace, and coworkers who are less familiar with their jobs need to fill in.

Morale

When employees are forced to take on more work due to absenteeism, they often become frustrated with their jobs. They resent management for the increased workload, and their morale decreases.

Trust

When employees are forced to take on more work due to absenteeism, they lose trust in management. The absenteeism is not their fault, yet they are paying the price. The worst part about issues involving trust is the fact that it is very difficult to restore once it is lost.

Stress

When employees are forced to take on more work due to absenteeism, they experience job stress. Over time, this causes them to burnout...and burnout causes their absenteeism to increase. It is rather ironic, but absenteeism results in absenteeism.

Turnover

When employees are forced to take on more work due to absenteeism, they start to dislike their jobs. This causes them to leave their organizations for other positions. In short, absenteeism results in turnover.

Now that you understand some of the more important effects of absenteeism, it is time to move into the next section that discusses methods of prevention.

Prevention

Once absenteeism starts, it can snowball and quickly get out of control. This is why the best way to stop it is to prevent it from occurring.

Some of the best methods of prevention include:

Hiring practices

Effective hiring practices are likely the best way to prevent absenteeism because (1) they prevent problem employees from entering the workplace and (2) they prevent employees from becoming problem employees.

The following are some important aspects of effective hiring practices:

Check references

It's always a good idea to call past employers to determine if potential employees have a history of absenteeism. It is illegal for employers to divulge certain facts about past employees, but they can release attendance records if policies were in place. This allows organizations to find out if potential employees were terminated for absenteeism related reasons.

Emphasize attendance importance

The importance of showing up for work should be stressed at the time of hiring. This makes it clear to employees that they are needed on the job and expected to show up when they are scheduled.

Orientation training

This occurs after the employee is hired. Orientation training talks about absenteeism and details the attendance policies in place...including disciplinary actions for violations. Training can be expensive, but it is well worth the cost if it is properly conducted.

Rewards

Rewards are a good way to prevent absenteeism because they provide goals and motivation for employees to show up for work.

There are several different types of rewards including:

Awards

Awards are typically certificates that commend good employee attendance. They are motivational because employees are recognized in front of the entire organization. They can also be used by employees for negotiating raises and other perks at a later time.

Incentive pay

This involves paying employees for good attendance. In other words, the incentive for reducing absenteeism is a cash reward. Typically, these are paid out on a monthly basis, and they can be in the form of an annual or bi-annual bonus.

Paid time off

Some organizations reward employees for good attendance by giving them paid time off. Certain workers prefer this over cash incentives because they value time more than additional income.

Lotteries

This involves lotteries for workers with good attendance. These individuals are entered in periodic (often monthly) lotteries with cash prizes that go to the selected winners.

All of the above rewards can be based on attendance systems put in place by organizations. For example, a system that issues employees points for unscheduled or unexcused absences could be utilized. Employees who reach a specified number of points are progressively disciplined...up to the point where they are terminated for extreme absenteeism.

Rewards can also be used to create peer pressure. Team or organization wide absenteeism systems can be put in place that document employee absenteeism as a whole. This results in employees monitoring each other's attendance because one employee's absenteeism can prevent everyone from receiving rewards.

Job rotation

This prevents absenteeism by (2) reducing the boredom of performing only one job and (2) empowering employees because they are more involved in the operation of the organization.

Another benefit is the fact employees know each other's jobs when someone is absent. This reduces mistakes and saves time in terms of training.

In short, job rotation reduces absenteeism because employees want to come to work, and they understand each other's jobs.

Communication

If absenteeism is an issue, management should ask employees why it is occurring. They might be surprised by the answers they receive from workers, and those answers can be used to prevent reoccurrences.

For example, some employees might indicate that they are missing time because other employees are always absent... and management does nothing about it. If this is the case, then an attendance system needs to be implemented.

As the saying goes, "a little communication goes a long way."

Summary

Absenteeism is employees' unscheduled absence from their jobs. Leaders of organizations generally do not have a problem with absenteeism unless it becomes excessive. Excessive absenteeism creates headaches for organizations because job tasks still need to be completed with fewer employees.

This eBook examines the causes and effects of absenteeism. It explores the reasons employees miss scheduled days of work, and it analyzes the problems this causes for organizations. It also offers suggestions for preventing workplace absenteeism so the negative effects can be minimized. Simple explanations are used for easy reader comprehension and understanding.

Congratulations! You now understand more about workplace absenteeism...and important aspect of organizational behavior.

www.ingramcontent.com/pod-product-compliance
Lightning Source LLC
Chambersburg PA
CBHW031547210526
45464CB00003B/1194